MW01233097

Gourmet Ghosts

(Pocket Guides)

Madness, Mayhem &
Strange Stories of Los Angeles

James T. Bartlett

City Ghost Guides

ISBN 978-09849730-4-0 (paperback)
ISBN 978-09849730-5-7 (ebook)

Gourmet Ghosts logo: U.S. Trademark No. 5,039,244

Introduction

I can't believe it has been over 10 years since I published *Gourmet Ghosts – Los Angeles*. I really didn't think that anyone would be interested in an odd guide to ghost stories at the bars, restaurants and hotels of L.A. – and I was completely wrong about that! People loved the true crimes too, and so that was the focus of *Gourmet Ghosts 2*.

In fact, one of the stories I found for *Gourmet Ghosts 2* intrigued me so much that it led me to write *The Alaskan Blonde: Sex, Secrets, and the Hollywood Story that Shocked America*, a true crime book which reexamines a murder that happened in Fairbanks, Alaska, in October 1953, and ended with a suicide at a hotel in Hollywood.

In the last few years, I have appeared with Zak Bagans on "Ghost Adventures" and on "The UnXplained with William Shatner", but I never stopped searching the archives, and I found so many weird stories that I wanted to share them – and I thought this pocket-sized guide might be the most fun way.

Please enjoy!

James T. Bartlett
Working at Central Library, Los Angeles
2023
www.gourmetghosts.com

Contents

Jack Morgan, the "Mad Pirate"

Date: December 24-30, 1937
Location: Catalina Island/Long Beach
Crimes: Mutiny, Murder, Kidnapping

When we think of a pirate, we prefer the swashbuckling yo-ho-ho *Pirates of the Caribbean* version, rather than the more modern *Captain Phillips* type, which involves motorboats of machine-gun desperadoes hijacking supertankers.

Even so, the idea of a pirate seems like something from very long ago – especially in America – so it's no surprise that around Christmas Day and through the last days of 1937, the story of "Mad" Jack Morgan captured headlines across America.

It seemed that everyone wanted to know about California's very own pirate, mutineer and maritime murderer.

He "blazed the bloodiest yachting trail in Southern California history," said the *LA Times* when it was reported that Morgan had met his death in exactly the way everyone might have imagined.

In the last desperate moments on board he was attacked by his prisoners, and thrown overboard to be eaten by sharks.

No one looked to see if he was alive or not.

The Pirate of Catalina Island

The rip-roaring tale of terror had begun on the serene waters around Santa Catalina Island, some 20 miles or so off the coast of Los Angeles, when 45-year-old Morgan chartered the 58-foot former racing schooner *Aafje* from Santa Barbara hotel owner Dwight L. Faulding.

AAFJE 1928

Morgan hired Faulding as skipper, and said he was planning a two-day pleasure cruise with his pregnant 18-year-old wife Lillian.

Also on the trip was Faulding's fiancée Gertrude Turner and her 8-year-old son Robert, plus Faulding's long-term crew employee Robert Horne.

Former high school football star George Spernak, 19, and 21-year-old nurse Elsie Berdan, who was to look after Lillian, rounded out the ocean-going party.

They set sail on December 20 from Long Beach, and it wasn't until they were several days overdue that Berdan's sister raised the alarm.

When police were told that Elsie had been kidnapped by Morgan, the FBI were bought into the case, and on December 30, it was reported that a naval plane had spotted the letters SOS on the sail of the *Aafje*, which was 180 miles south of Long Beach or, in some reports, "drifting 300 miles off the coast of Mexico."

Sounding The Alarm

Coast Guard cutter *Perseus* was dispatched, and they found the *Aafje*'s mainsail broken and the engine out of fuel, so they began towing the blood-stained vessel back to Long Beach, and an FBI agent took a motorboat to meet the "yacht of death."

SLEUTH ON WAY TO DEATH YACHT

The exhausted passengers were hungry and shaken but otherwise unhurt, but both Faulding and Jack Morgan were missing. What had happened?

On New Year's Eve, the public learned the sensational truth. Just off Catalina, Faulding and Morgan got into an argument and Morgan shot his captain in the shoulder.

Wincing in pain, Faulding tried to cool things down, saying: "Be a good fellow and put that gun away. We're all out for a good time."

Unsurprisingly, Faulding then went to get his .38, but when Morgan appeared on the stairs above him, he opened fire. Morgan shot back five times, hitting Faulding in the heart and killing him instantly.

Morgan ordered Faulding's body weighted with an anchor and thrown overboard, closed the yacht's hatches, and locked the passengers in their cabins.

Wrecked At Sea

Over the next few days, Morgan roughed up the men, withheld food, and grandly assumed the role of captain. He talked of his wild plans to head for the South Seas, raiding ports for supplies en route.

On Christmas Eve, Spernak and Horne saw their chance for freedom. Horne attacked with a wooden marlin spike, and then the pair threw him over the side too, not caring that sharks would be attracted by his bleeding injuries.

Mad Pirate Is Slain By Yacht Crew

Whether Morgan was alive when he hit the water was never revealed, but the "Mad Pirate" was now deep in Davy Jones' Locker, and Spernak and Horne were arrested as soon as they set foot back on land.

Morgan's Murder?

Waiting in the crowd were members of the Faulding family, who had expected to collect Dwight's body for burial; they left in tears. Lillian Morgan, her head bandaged, was held as a material witness too, and a grand jury was assembled.

Charged with murder on the high seas, the two young men were going to plead self-defense and remanded overnight in the County Jail, but no one thought the case would even come to trial, especially when Elsie told reporters that Morgan was "the cruelest man I ever knew."

Elsie (left) and her sister, who called the police

She also said that Lillian had tried to restrain her husband, but he treated her "inhumanely," forcing her to hold everyone at gunpoint when he wanted to sleep, and threatening to kill her if she refused. Elsie added that Morgan made "improper advances to her, bordering on the erotic."

Spernak and Horne had led the attempt to sail back to Long Beach, and were duly unanimously freed by the grand jury – as was Lillian Morgan.

Who Was Morgan?

Tall and handsome with a pencil mustache, Morgan had a colorful past. Born in Nicaragua to French and German parents as Jean Dee Barnette, he had come to with them to California as a child, and ran away to sea soon after. He then worked on vessels around the world – when he wasn't spending years behind bars.

He had convictions for sexual assault, burglary and petty theft, and had only been released from San Quentin Prison earlier in 1937, soon after which he and Lillian had eloped from New Orleans. Lillian's father had not heard from her since that day – until now.

Time magazine wrote a detailed summary of events, and the

LA Times wondered if Morgan was related to the infamous Sir Henry Morgan, who terrorized the Spanish Main in the 17th century (and inspired the famous rum).

He wasn't, though that didn't stop one of the many pulp magazines of the era putting him on their front cover.

Intrigued by its dark past, actor Errol Flynn (right), famous for playing a pirate called *Captain Blood*, was rumored to have considered buying the abandoned *Aafje*, but instead screenwriter John Taintor Foote (*The Story of Seabiscuit*) was seemingly the very last official owner.

Sadly, the yacht's tragic story never made it to the big screen, and that might have been because the glamour of the illegal casino boats that moored off the California coast the following year overshadowed it.

A month after the eight-day "battle" between the *SS Rex* and the police in Santa Monica Bay, World War II broke out in Europe, and that more or less ensured the terrible story of "Mad" Jack Morgan sailed quietly into history.

L.A's very own "Bonnie & Clyde"

Date: November 1930 – January 1931
Location: Various across Los Angeles
Crimes: Robbery, Assault, Attempted Murder

Several years before the deadly escapades of Bonnie and Clyde thrilled America, two young, star-crossed lovers named Lucille Walker and Alexander Mackay led a six-week rampage of robberies across Los Angeles.

From Thanksgiving 1930, they and their gang committed almost 40 hold-ups at drug stores and hotels, the city's newspapers relishing every moment of it, especially the story of a seemingly-innocent young woman drawn into a life of crime.

When she was first captured in January 1931, 19-year-old Lucille Walker was christened the "Red-Haired Bandit Queen" by the *Los Angeles Times*.

She seemed far from being an innocent though, and she brazenly admitted to reporters that she planned and took part in nearly all the robberies – though the truth was rather different.

The Oklahoma-born "Queen of Crooks" called her arrest, for trying to buy a pistol with the 23-year-old MacKay, a "tough break," and that her first robbery was "exciting."

However, she denied using a gun during the crimes: instead, she said she pointed her finger in her pocket, making it look like a weapon, and insisted that no-one was ever hurt.

Also, despite her exotic media nickname, Lucille was actually a blonde. She had dyed her eyebrows and lashes black and wore a red wig for a while, changing it to a brunette one when the police got on her tail – and she happily showed photographers how she did it.

She further explained that she used to work the soda fountain at a drug store, and it was here that she studied the cash till, and how the store distributed and handled money. But then, in debt and out of work, she met MacKay at a dance hall.

In a moment straight out of a movie, he asked her if she "had any nerve," and she replied that yes, she did. Their criminal career was off and running – at least for a while.

Arrested

In March, Otis Saunders, 21, had three guns in his car when he was stopped by police in San Jose, and it emerged that while he, Lucille and MacKay had indeed robbed the Gaylord Hotel on Wilshire Boulevard among others, it was Saunders and two other men who had attacked the Gotham Hotel in downtown L.A.

Hotel Gotham, Los Angeles   65491

975 Ingraham St. between Seventh and Wilshire. One Block West of Figueroa St.   65491

Lucille and Mackay had also been arrested after the Gotham robbery, but as part of a round-up of the "usual suspects", and since several people at the Gotham had been injured by gunfire and the criminal charges were likely to be more serious, Lucille now began to change her tune.

She Didn't Really Want To Do It

Saunders was the real mastermind behind the dozens of robberies she insisted, and in fact MacKay had threatened Lucille and her mother, saying that they would both be "taken for a ride" if she didn't join up and play bandit.

In what seemed to be a romantic jailhouse gesture, MacKay nobly confirmed these allegations and swore that Lucille was completely innocent.

'Just Made Fair Living'

LUCILLE WALKER (alias Lucille Gordon), who admitted to police she took part in 25 store robberies, and highlights in her career.—Examiner photo.

She further insisted that she hadn't got rich from her nefarious deeds anyway; she just got "room and board, a dress, hat, silk stocking and a $12 pair of shoes," and had just made what she called a "fair living" at her life of crime.

She also made an appeal to any soft-hearted newspaper readers – and future jurors – by saying that she sent $2,000 to her mother.

Even so, the jury took barely 20 minutes to find her guilty of involvement in three robberies, and Judge Walton J. Wood chastised MacKay and the lawyers for trying to exonerating Lucille.

It was "utterly silly" and "an insult to the intelligence," he thundered.

Prison Time

Both were sentenced to five years to life in the notorious San Quentin State Prison in San Francisco, though Lucille was transferred to Tehachapi Prison in southern California in in November 1933, and, unusually, had been allowed to apply for probation.

Lucille Walker
alias
Lucille Gordon —
Robb 1 at 3 cts cc —
L.a. — 5 to Life 3 cts
cc — Okla — 20 —
Waitress — 5'1'1/4" —
Comp Fair — Eyes
Gry — Hair Blonde
133. Rec'd 4/15/31.   1 ʊ Ⅱ 8
Trans 11/7/33 to   1 ʊ ʊⅠ 5
Tehachapi. Par L/19-34.
. Wanted, Robbery, Los A. Police Bull. 2/1/35.

It was an extremely rare occurrence for someone convicted of such crimes, and it proved to be a hasty decision by the authorities, as a note on her prison record indicated that after her release she went back to her wicked ways, and was wanted for robbery in Los Angeles in February 1935.

MacKay's Escape Plan

She never saw Alex Mackay again: just a few weeks before she was freed from Tehachapi, he was part of a four-man team that tried to escape from San Quentin.

Alongside Joe Kristy and Fred Landers, Mackay had been working in the prison grounds on a building near prison warden James B. Holohan's home, and serial escapee Ronald Straight quickly saw this as a route to escape.

Using guns smuggled into the prison, Straight joined the others in the truck driving to the work site and, unnoticed by two guards, they entered the warden's house where Holohan was meeting with the members of the State Board of Prison Terms and Paroles.

Straight slugged Holohan with his revolver, fracturing his skull, and the plan was that they would take Holohan and several members of the Board as hostage when they made their way north in Holohan's car. The gang switched clothes with the Board members, and took the two guards with them for good measure: they now had six men as human shields.

Chased by prison guards and state highway police, they were finally trapped some 40 miles away at Valley Ford, where a posse was waiting for them and opened fire. The gang abandoned the bullet-ridden car for refuge in a nearby creamery, and a gun battle followed. Straight tried to shoot his way out and was killed, upon which the other three men surrendered.

Convicts Confess Secrets of Daring Escape Plot

The escape was a sensation, the *Los Angeles Evening-Post Record* showing the three dejected escapees back in prison, and a smiling Houlahan in his hospital bed.

Despite being given the Last Rites Houlahan made a full recovery, and the next year he discussed his experiences in a series for the *Los Angeles Times* called "My San Quentin Years".

While Fred Landers was sentenced to life with the possibility for parole because he had tried to stop Straight beating Holohan further, MacKay and Kristy turned a similar kidnapping with violence plea deal down. With a touch of admiration, Holohan noted that Mackay said:

> *"Of the two – the noose or slow death in prison – I'd rather have the last one."*

Both he and Joe Kristy were in due course tried and sentenced to death, but Holohan knew nothing of the international incident that was brewing when he got a call from England – at a whopping $13 a minute ($262 today).

Perhaps foolishly, he allowed Mackay to be interviewed on the phone by the *London News Chronicle*, and it emerged that Mackay had written to the Houses of Parliament in London.

Born in Govan, a suburb of Glasgow, Scotland, Mackay was a British citizen, and was now appealing to the authorities in his homeland to help him get clemency.

Over the next few weeks and months, various individuals of the British Government tried to intercede on Mackay's behalf, arguing that the death penalty was "unnecessary severe." Mackay also argued that the robbery convictions he got alongside Lucille in Los Angelee were unjust, and so he had every right to try and escape.

The Man Who Wrote to the King of England

However, all the political and diplomatic fury – appeals to California's Governor and State Supreme Court, and even Mackay asking his lawyer to write to England's new King Edward VIII to ask for his personal intervention – came to nothing.

A late plea via the Canadian Prime Minister from MacKay's mother, who lived in Montreal, didn't stop the route to the gallows either.

"QUEEN OF CROOKS" ADMITS ROBBERIES

All hope surely disappeared when, just a few days later, the District Attorney who tried Mackay and Kristy received a letter threatening death to him and his family unless he did "everything in is power" to stop the executions.

So, despite the various pleas and stays, both Mackay and Kristy were executed on May 22, 1936.

Warden Holohan, who had watched 57 men executed during his time at San Quentin, excused himself that day: as he told readers of the *Los Angeles Times*, "it might have seemed like personal vengeance."

Lucille's reaction to her one-time lover's death is unknown, and there were no other references to the 1935 robbery allegation in police records.

By then the shocking murder/robbery spree of two other young, gun-toting lovers – Bonnie Parker and Clyde Barrow – had been seared into the American consciousness, and this surely helped the one-time "Queen of Crooks" disappear into history...

Halloween Murders

Dates: 1967, 1974, 1957
Locations: Van Nuys, Chinatown, Sun Valley
Crimes: Murder

You would think that Halloween was the perfect time to carry out a murder. It's the one day and night of the year when you can walk around in disguise, even carry a gun or a bloody knife, and no one will be suspicious.

Even so, the newspaper archives only revealed a few murders that had actually taken place on Halloween, the 31st of October – though two of them really did make use of crazy costumes to cover up their deadly intentions.

On April 26, 1969 the *LA Times* reported how 35-year-old car salesman Jack Gentry Stearns had been found guilty of shooting 32-year-old Kenneth A. Lindstrand in front of dozens of witnesses at Country Club Halloween costume party in Van Nuys on Halloween night in 1967.

Lindstrand was one of the few people not in costume, and so when a man also not in costume ran after him shooting a gun, people thought it was a prank. One woman in a hula skirt even began to dance over Lindstrand's body saying "This will wake him up" – until she realized he was dead!

Defendant in 1967 Halloween Party Murder Sentenced to Life

Stearns had apparently objected to the way Lindstrand was dancing with his wife Maria, and was sent to prison for life.

3 Trick-or-Treat Terrorists Kill Man, 81, in Chinatown Home

A much scarier headline was the "3 Trick or Treat Terrorists" one, which reported on a murder that took place around 9pm on Halloween Night 1974 when elderly Mrs. Low answered the door of her Chinatown home to three masked "trick or treaters".

She recalled that one of them was wearing a wolfman mask, another Frankenstein, but they all pointed guns at her and forced their way into the house, but when nearly-blind 81-year-old Pok Suey Low came out from the bedroom, one of them shot him in the chest.

The teenagers fled, leaving behind several masks and – bizarrely – a large bag of candy and chocolates.

In February the following year, two 15-year-old boys confessed to the crime when they were caught after beating, robbing and kidnapping a 20-year-old man named Chan Wing Wong from Lincoln Heights.

They drove him out to San Bernardino, telling him they were going to bury his body in Cajon Pass, but luckily Wong escaped and raised the alarm.

Ghost Killer

Perhaps the craziest of the Halloween murders I found happened on 31st October 1957, and was another "trick or treat" scam killing.

TRICK, TREAT GUNMAN MURDERS L.A. MAN

In this case 35-year-old beauty shop owner Peter Fabiano answered the door of his Sun Valley home to two people dressed in costumes and was then shot once, dying later in hospital.

In March the next year, 43-year-old medical clerk Goldyne Pizer (right; who looks SO happy in this photo) and 40-year-old photographer Joan Rabel (with her lawyer, left) pleaded guilty to second degree murder.

WOMEN CHANGE PLEAS TO GUILTY.
2 Admit Halloween Killing

In a sudden switch, Joan Rabel, 46, and Goldine Pizer, 43, pleaded guilty yesterday to the Halloween "trick-or-treat" murder of beauty parlor operator Peter Fabiano, 35.

The two women, after meeting with their attorney, admitted guilt when Deputy District Attorney Joseph Carr agreed to reduce the charges against them to second degree murder.

They were returned to await sentence April 4. Each faces a five-year-to-life prison term.

SHOT AT DOOR—

Fabiano was shot by a masked, Halloween-attired woman when he answered the doorbell at his home, 13236 Community street, Sun Valley.

Officers learned that Mrs. Rabel, a former cafe photographer, was an intimate friend of Fabiano's wife, Betty, and had upbraided Mrs. Fabiano for returning to him following a separation.

But, it was Mrs. Pizer, a hospital clerk, who told the startling story of committing the murder at Mrs. Rabel's suggestion, after they bought a gun and borrowed a cat from a friend.

Mrs. Pizer, police said, admitted being dominated by Mrs. Rabel, who spent three

GOLDINE PIZER
She faces prison term.

months inquiring in her mind a hatred for Fabiano whom she had never met.

2 Billion for Foreign Travel

WASHINGTON, March 11 (INS)—The Commerce Department reported today United States residents spent nearly $2,000,000,000 for foreign travel in 1957.

JOAN RABEL CONFERS WITH HER ATTORNEY
Ralph Rosenstock counseled her in her plea.

21

Goldyne – who had dressed in a white sheet as a ghost – was the one who pulled the trigger, firing from inside her handbag, and she told the jury that Rabel had spent nearly three months persuading her to hate Fabiano.

They had taken joint trips to his beauty salon to have their hair done – and so that Goldyne knew what he looked like – and it seemed that Goldyne was the easily-manipulated pasty in the diabolical scheme.

The motive? Joan Rabel was once a good friend of Fabiano's wife Betty, but was none too pleased Betty had let her husband back into her life after a temporary separation.

Was this her misguided way to try and "free" Betty from what she saw as a bad marriage, or maybe there was more to it than that – Jealousy? Secret love? Either way, Goldyne and Rabel were both sentenced to five years to life.

Stepping into the Void

Dates: 1896-1948

Locations: Downtown and Hollywood

Suddenly, you're falling, falling, falling. You barely have a few seconds to realize what's happening – maybe your shout or scream echoes for a moment – before you come to a hard, bone-crunching death in the darkness.

For many people, the idea of falling down an elevator shaft – or getting caught or crushed in the doors – is the ultimate nightmare, even if such accidents are very rare in modern times.

However, the archives revealed that a hundred years or so ago, such horrors were far more common than we might think, especially in hotels and multi-storey buildings.

There are a couple of reasons for this. Firstly, in the early days many people were not used to elevators, which is why there were official operators.

They often had pull-down or concertina metal gates, maybe no roof, and they weren't automated either, meaning that the doors didn't open and close only when they reached a floor, nor did electric sensors re-open doors instantly if someone tried to get in or out.

Also, many elevators were controlled by a simple stop-and-go lever, and, believe it or not, the massive counterweights often weren't encased far away from the carriage.

However, sometimes people were just suicidally curious about looking into dark shafts, or wanted to try and joke around, or simply didn't look before they stepped into the carriage.

Unfortunately, sometimes it in hadn't arrived yet, or had under or overshot the stop, or had been delayed for another reason – and arrived at just the wrong time.

The occasional lucky survivor of an elevator shaft falls often sued for damages, which is probably part of the reason they became safer. But many did not, and these are the stories – an unlucky 13 of them – that I found.

Van Nuys Hotel
103 4th St
March 4, 1897
One of the oldest hotels in Los Angeles, the Van Nuys became the Barclay Hotel in 1929, and those signs still adorn what is now low-income housing – though architecture and windows still show the last name of Isaac Van Nuys, the Los Angeles pioneer and original owner.

However, just months after the hotel opened, hotel

waiter Charles G. Gamble and the elevator boy, Robert White, were going down to the first floor and "joking" together when White turned the lever the wrong way, and it began going up again.

Having "lost their presence of mind," White jumped out of the still-moving elevator at the third floor and Gamble, apparently frightened, tried to follow him out – but too late.

Caught in the doorway, the rising elevator then pinned his legs, which "snapped like pipestems…"

MANGLED BEFORE HE FELL.

TERRIBLE ACCIDENT AT THE NEW VAN NUYS HOTEL.

The *Los Angeles Times* went on to graphically describe how Gamble's body was dragged up by the foot until "that was smashed" and he fell head-first to his death, his skull fractured in multiple places and his left eye actually torn from the socket.

Amazingly Gamble was still alive, but "after nearly an hour of intense suffering," he died in hospital.

Van Nuys Hotel
January 3, 1900
Tragedy came to the hotel again early in the new millennium, when bell boy Earl Newton, aged just 16, was on top of the elevator cage when he accidentally pulled on the power rope, causing the elevator to rise and trap him between the shaft and the ceiling on that floor.

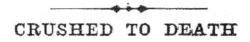

CRUSHED TO DEATH

Horrifyingly, it was reported that his internal organs were instantly crushed, and the blood rushing to his head turned his face purple.

Van Nuys Hotel
September 21, 1901
It was third time unlucky for Joe Kato, a Japanese assistant janitor at the hotel. He couldn't help his curiosity about the open elevator shaft, and peeked into the darkness.

Predictably – and horribly – he was hit on the head by the 4800lb counter weight that went down as the elevator went up, and he was killed instantly.

Hellman Building

411 S Main St

February 8, 1905

Tulsi Indian restaurant is on the street level here at the Hellman, which was originally the location of banker Herman Hellman's home before it became a major building in 1903.

In 1905, head janitor Chris Larsen was hit by the descending cage of the building elevator, and killed instantly.

Brains Strewn Down Shaft.

HORRID ACCIDENT IN HELLMAN BUILDING ELEVATOR.

"Nearly the whole top of his head was torn off, and the unfortunate man's brains and blood were spattered along the sides of the elevator shaft from the fifth floor to the basement."

Larsen had been standing on the top of another elevator cage, cleaning the ironwork on the inside of the shaft, and had leaned out several times.

He had been warned to be careful, but instead he just laughed off any concerns – a decision that was deadly for him.

Bradbury Building
November 22, 1908
304 S Broadway

The head janitor was looking for his assistant, 34-year-old Carl King, but couldn't find him – until he looked down the elevator shaft and saw his body, which had been there for several hours.

King's skull had been crushed and many bones broken, and it emerged that he probably got caught between the 2nd and 3rd floors, and had been hurled about 35 feet to his death.

Alexandria Hotel
501 S Spring St
December 22, 1910

Two men were killed and two injured when the platform they were standing on in the elevator shaft, which also had barrels of plaster on it, collapsed.

Ernest Pearman and Joseph Lawrence, both plasterers, fell seven floors; Pearman's skull was crushed and he died at the scene, but Pearman, also with a skull fracture and several ribs puncturing his liver, lingered for several hours in hospital.

The other two men, Stephen Smith and Charles Lentz, managed to grab something and save themselves; they only suffered cuts and bruises.

Douglas Building
257 S Spring St

Built in 1898, today the Douglas Building is a loft development, and I have a friend who lives in one of the apartments.

I told her that three employees of her building had died in the elevator there – just like at the Van Nuys Hotel. Shocked, she said she would be taking the stairs from now on.

December 20, 1905

Clifford J Rudd, engineer of the Douglas Building for the past four years, entered the counterweight shaft and stood on a small platform he had constructed to adjust the tension of cables.

Awful Fate That Befell the Assistant Engineer of the Douglas Block Yesterday Morning.

The elevator car was at the bottom of the shaft, and what happened next was unknown, but his body was found lying across an iron beam, crushed under that counterweight.

March 31, 1941

80-year-old elevator operator WP Brown ran to get into the elevator – but was too late. He missed the carriage and fell three floors down the shaft to his death. Apparently he had been unwell

February 18, 1948

John Goris, a 50-year-old carpenter, was decapitated when the elevator balance weight struck him on the back of the neck.

He had been working on an elevator repair, and put his head through a hole in a wall – and was hit by the weight.

Roosevelt Building
727 W 7th St
January 7, 1927

Laborer R. Ponce, 45, slipped into an empty elevator shaft and fell eight storeys to his death.

Spring Arts Tower
453 S Spring St
July 4, 1927

During research for *Gourmet Ghosts – Los Angeles*, I spoke to Kevin Taylor, a history graduate and former manager of the Spring Arts Tower.

He had researched the building and had a number of ghost stories, the most chilling of which was one about a ghostly figure going around opening and closing doors on the 3rd floor, and how he heard a sound of jingling keys, like a watchman was on duty:

"I heard the keys myself, and was spooked because I was the only one at the time who had a set of keys for the building. In fact, one of the workers heard the jingling keys up there just a couple of weeks back."

Soon after, I uncovered an articles in the *Los Angeles Times* and *Los Angeles Examiner* archives that revealed there had indeed been a tragic accident here – and not only on the 3rd floor, but the victim was the building watchman!

Employees at the Citizens National Bank, the ground floor tenant (now the Crocker Club), had heard a man groaning around 10am the morning of the previous day, but could not find anyone in distress.

The next day it was revealed that sometime during the previous night watchman Al Brietenbecker had fallen from the 3rd floor down the freight elevator shaft – which had no roof – to the sub-basement, severing a major artery in the fall.

Evidence showed that he tried frantically to staunch the flow of blood with torn pieces of his own clothing, but his efforts were unsuccessful and his dead body was found around midday.

The freight elevator is off-limits to the public, but the famous building tenant – The Last Bookstore – has let me take walking tours in there, and I promise you that it's a creepy feeling to step inside!

Spring Arcade
541 S Spring St
January 30, 1946

Ernest C. Bean, 55, an employee for the Spring Arcade, tried to jump onto a sidewalk elevator in the basement, but mistimed his jump and was killed instantly when his body was crushed against an overhead beam.

Christie Hotel
6724 Hollywood Blvd
September 1, 1943

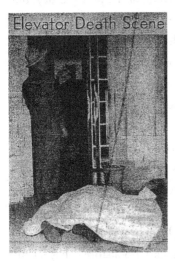

Albert Bellerose, 28, an elevator operator who had only worked at the Christie for three days, was killed – his head and neck "crushed" – when he was dragged into the narrow space between the lift and the shaft.

Witnesses heard a short scream, and saw his legs extending from the top of the elevator door.

The fire department had to be called to "extricate his body."

Murder in my Neighborhood

Date: June 30, 1959
Location: 129 N Oxford Ave
Crime: Double Murder

Whenever I hear about a new hotel or a bar opening, I always look up the address in the newspaper archives, because you never know what might crime or tragedy – or ghost sighting – might have happened there in days gone by.

Actually, no matter where I go I always make sure to keep an eye out for anything unusual or different, and the same goes for my own neighborhood.

I was out jogging the other evening when I went past a very funky looking building that had a dotty color scheme and a very memorable porch and doorway.

When I got home I looked up the address online to see if there was anything interesting about it – maybe the architect was someone notable? – and was amazed at what I found.

On June 30, 1959, 52-year-old Lillian Engel, a secretary for the IRS, and her (presumed boyfriend) Sumner Packard, 53, a city engineering inspector, were moving out of their apartment here when tragedy came to call at the front door.

Packard was approached by Elmer Engel, who opened fire and shot Packard in the heart, killing him instantly.

Elmer then went into the apartment, locked the door, and shot Lillian in the head before turning the .32 caliber pistol on himself. In just a few seconds, three people were dead.

Triple Slaying Comes as Pair Prepares to Move to Avoid Jealous Former Husband

During the investigation that followed, a lawyer admitted that a restraining order had previously been filed against Elmer, who had allegedly been physically abusive to Lillian, but – as if often the case in domestic violence case – he had always tracked her down.

She had even moved home several times to try and stop Elmer from finding her, but he always did. This move was her latest attempt to try and start over, but unfortunately, it was also the last.

It was a sad tale for sure, but then the report revealed that Packard, the boyfriend who seemed to have been in the wrong place at the wrong time, had a strange story of his own.

He was known to others in the building not as Sumner Packard, but as "Thomas Perkins". More than that, it seemed that he had initially been living there with his ex-wife Georgia, who he had been trying to commit to a mental institution, and that Lillian had moved in recently.

Packard/Perkins also apparently owned and lived at an apartment building in Burbank, where residents knew nothing of another girlfriend, let alone his apparently secret life with her!

A real murder/mystery then, and another example of the old adage that you never know what happens behind closed doors...

Hollywood Forever & Ever?

Date: June 24, 1953

Location: Hollywood Forever, 6000 Santa Monica Blvd

Also in my neighborhood is Hollywood Forever, a 62-acre cemetery, funeral home, crematory and events center that sits alongside (and once used to be a part) of Paramount Studios.

Unmissable whether you're in town for a visit – or have just never been here before – it's the resting place of countless celebrities from the last 100 years.

Everyone from Douglas Fairbanks, Rudolph Valentino, Cecil B DeMille, Judy Garland, Burt Reynolds, voice genius Mel Blanc, musicians Chris Cornell and Dee Dee Ramone and – most recently – actresses Anne Heche and Kirstine Alley are here.

Gangster Bugsy Siegel is too, and several other notable murder victims or scandalized people from years gone by.

Not only that, you'll also find countless squirrels hopping and skittering around, a healthy population of cemetery cats – some of which might let you pet them – and a large number of magnificent peacocks and peahens, who stroll majestically around like they own the place.

There's also a triangle-shaped crypt, a statue of a dog ("Toto"), a memorial to the victims of the 1910 bombing of the *Los Angeles Times*, and a mausoleum that contains the remains of one of the child survivors of the *Titanic* sinking in 1912.

Unusually, Hollywood Forever has also been the place where someone committed suicide – and it was all a part of his plan to visit the afterlife.

Englishman Cyril Thorne had been fascinated by psychic phenomena for years, and when his first wife Addie died in 1946 aged just 38, she was buried at Hollywood Forever (though in those days it was called Hollywood Memorial Park).

Dinner with the Dead

He married again, but wife #2 Joan understandably filed for divorce when he started setting an extra place at the dinner table for the late Addie: he was firm in his belief that she was still a presence in his life – and the marital home.

A few years after that in 1952, Thorne married to wife #3, whose name was Jean, in Las Vegas.

However, his obsession with Addie had not changed, and on the evening of June 24, 1953, Thorne went to Hollywood Memorial.

He bought a large bunch of flowers, and made his way to her marble grave (Section 13, Lot 850, #5). He was carrying a photograph of him and wife #3

Jean on their wedding day, and a briefcase containing a carbon monoxide cylinder and mask, and a pile of typewritten notes.

One of them was to Jean, who he wrote was a "very perfect, dependable and lovely wife," and read in part:

> "My research into the study of psychic phenomena has brought me to the place where I am better than 50 percent convinced that death does not mean the end of this entity we call 'I'".

Another of the notes contained detailed instructions for his non-religious funeral service, which was to be conducted by the wonderfully-named Dr. Hereward Carrington from the American Psychical Institute.

Once beside the grave he sat down, put on the mask, and turned on the carbon monoxide cylinder. It emerged that he had used this method to attempt suicide before, but this time he was sure that he would be able to reach back from the afterlife.

Another note requested that:

> "Some light, tall object be placed on top of the coffin in full view of everyone. ... I will try to knock it off if I can. If I don't succeed, it will prove nothing to those of you who do not understand. If I do, it will prove much."

After the service was over, the curious crowd – including Jean and Cyril's mother and sister – remained to see if, just maybe, the cardboard cylinder or plastic object Carrington placed on top of the coffin would move.

NO SIGN FROM BEYOND
Suicide's Spirit Fails to Return at Funeral

Of course, despite Carrington urging "Cy" to reach out from beyond, there was no signal. Perhaps Cyril was so happy to be reunited with his beloved Addie that he forgot to signal his friends back in Hollywood – though his note to Jean also said "Good night... until we meet again."

This odd tale of life after death is reminiscent of the story of Harry Houdini, the legendary escapologist and a fervent disbeliever in the then-popular fashion of seances, where you were supposed to be able to contact the dead.

He died on Halloween night 1926 (of course he did), but he had already told his wife Beatrice that, if there was in fact anything in the afterlife, he would contact her.

The devoted Beatrice held séances every Halloween for the next ten years in an attempt to contact him, the last taking place with much publicity on the roof of the Knickerbocker Hotel in Hollywood (less than a mile and half from Hollywood Forever).

Perhaps inevitably, the afterlife was one thing that Houdini couldn't escape from. As she snuffed out the candle, Beatrice sadly said:

"Ten years is long enough to wait for any man."

Jack the Ripper – in Los Angeles?

Dates: 1888, 1892
Location: Liverpool, London, Los Angeles?
Crimes: Deception/Theft, Multiple Murder?

Several killers like the Night Stalker, the Grim Sleeper, the Golden State Killer, and the infamous Charles Manson and his Family have haunted California and especially Los Angeles over the last few decades.

Hollywood screenwriters have loved serial killers too, but since the 1920s they have sent the most famous of them, Jack the Ripper, everywhere from the future to outer space.

Film database IMDB.com lists over 100 productions in every conceivable genre about or related to Jack the Ripper, with perhaps the most high-profile big version being 2001 *From Hell* starring Johnny Depp.

Around the time of the Ripper's killings in the East End district of Whitechapel in London in 1888, Sir Arthur Conan-Doyle, the creator of Sherlock Holmes, expressed the opinion that Jack might have spent time in America.

Even so, a direct connection between Los Angeles and the Ripper isn't immediately apparent – until now.

In the archives I uncovered newspaper reports suggesting that Jack may indeed have visited L.A. – and claimed another victim there.

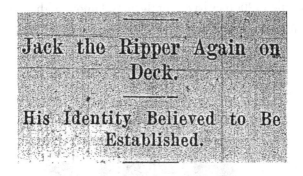

That was the headline in the *Los Angeles Herald* of March 17, 1892, which reported that an Englishman named Williams had been arrested in Australia, and charged with murdering his wife at their home in Melbourne.

Williams had previously lived near Liverpool, where workmen found the buried bodies of his former wife and three children, all killed by strangulation or having their throats cut. In the wife's arms was a small baby, its head crushed in.

"I am Jack the...."

Williams' real name was Frederick Bailey Deeming, and he had a long history of travelling the world committing crimes of bigamy, theft and deception, something that the *Los Angeles Herald* noted alongside the fact that, just before he swung from the hangman's noose, he had confessed to two of the Ripper's murders in Whitechapel.

Soon after, the *Los Angeles Times* of April 17, 1892 wondered whether "this fiend in human form" had lived in Los Angeles before he fled to England and began his infamous murdering spree.

A story from April 1888 – nearly four months before the first murder in Whitechapel – reported that a Charles H. Williams had married, scammed, and robbed Nannie Catching, a music teacher and singer living in downtown L.A.

A MUSIC TEACHER FALLS INTO THE HANDS OF A FAKIR.

Despite her friend's advice Nannie had quickly married the charming "Charles" in January 1888, though strangely there were no wedding photos – the groom apparently hated having his picture taken. A few months later, she came home to find a note saying he had gone away on business, and then she found all her money (around $2,500 – well over $70,000 today) was gone too.

Sensing a scoop, the *Times* excitedly reported that there were notable absences in Deeming's whereabouts from 1886 to 1888, and over the next few days it reported that several people had seen a picture of Deeming, and they felt certain that the Charles Williams they knew in L.A. was the same man.

Christened an "unmitigated scoundrel" by the Los Angeles newspapers, the only evidence they had of what Charles looked like were photographic illustrations of him.

The best of the illustrations shows "Charles Williams" on the left, while Deeming's real photograph is on the right.

That they both had big mustaches might seem just a coincidence, but there were other links between Deeming and Charles. Charles told friends he was from Australia for example, and he had drunkenly boasted about seducing women out of their money.

He was also said to have a nasty temper, and was always changing his life story. Both men were Masons too, and both had showcased their excellent singing voices in church services.

Deeming was NOT Jack – but Charles…?

As intriguing as this all seems, it's accepted today among historians and Ripperologists that Frederick Deeming definitely wasn't Jack the Ripper.

However, that certainly doesn't necessarily mean that Deeming never visited Los Angeles, nor that Nannie had a lucky escape from someone who was a mass murderer-to-be, just not the one we all came to know as "Jack."

Unsurprisingly, the L.A. "connection" disappeared from the headlines after Deeming's execution, but a copy of his death mask was still shipped to Scotland Yard's famous Black Museum after his death, where for years it was nevertheless introduced to visitors as "the death mask of Jack the Ripper."

About The Author

Originally from London, James T. Bartlett has been living in Los Angeles since 2004.

As a travel and lifestyle journalist and historian, he has written for the Los Angeles Times, BBC, Los Angeles Magazine, ALTA Journal, Hemispheres, Westways, Frommers, American Way, Crime Reads, Atlas Obscura, Real Crime, The Guardian, Career Authors, Variety, Bizarre, History Ireland, and the Whitechapel Journal, among others.

In 2012 he wrote *Gourmet Ghosts – Los Angeles*, an alternative guide to the history and ghost stories behind some of the city's oldest bars, restaurants and hotels, while *Gourmet Ghosts 2* (2016) focused on true crimes that took place at more of L.A.'s notable locations and eateries.

The books led to lectures, events, true crime book club hosting and appearances on radio, podcasts, and television programs including *Ghost Adventures* and *The UnXplained*.

He is also the author of *The Alaskan Blonde: Sex, Secrets, and the Hollywood Story that Shocked America*, a true crime book reexamining a scandalous 1953 murder that began in Alaska and ended in Hollywood, while his short story "Death

Under the Stars" was included in the recent Sisters in Crime Los Angeles anthology *Entertainment To Die For.*

You can find out more information at www.gourmetghosts.com or www.thealaskanblonde.com and you can email James at jbartlett2000@gmail.com

Made in the USA
Monee, IL
17 October 2024